What Can We Play Today?

by Jane Belk Moncure
illustrated by Linda Hohag

Published by

Mankato, Minnesota

GROLIER
B O O K S

Grolier Books is a division of
Grolier Enterprises, Inc.,
Danbury, CT.

The Library— A Magic Castle

Come to the magic castle
When you are growing tall.
Rows upon rows of Word Windows
Line every single wall.
They reach up high,
As high as the sky,
And you want to open them all.
For every time you open one,
A new adventure has begun.

Lisa opens a Word Window.
Here's what she reads.

What can we play today? We can
play "dress-up." Look in the
"dress-up" box. What do you see?

Can you guess who we will be?
We will be fire fighters, that's who.

What do fire fighters do? They put out
fires. That's what they do.

Get the ladder. Get the hose. Swish.
Out the fire goes.

forest fire

factory fire

boat fire

Fire fighters fight all kinds of fires.

Look in the box again. What do you see? Can you guess who we will be?

Police officers, that's who. What do
police officers do? They help keep
us safe wherever we go.

Police officers help us know when
to stop and when to go.

And when someone is in trouble,
police officers come "on the double."

Look in the box again. What do you see? Can you guess who we will be?

A doctor and a nurse, that's who.
What do doctors and nurses do?

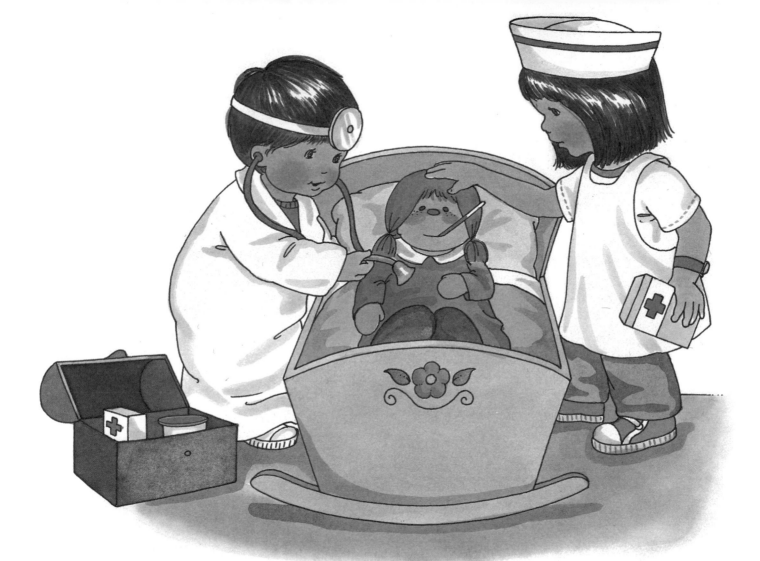

They take care of sick people.
That's what they do.

family doctor

school nurse

Doctors and nurses help people stay

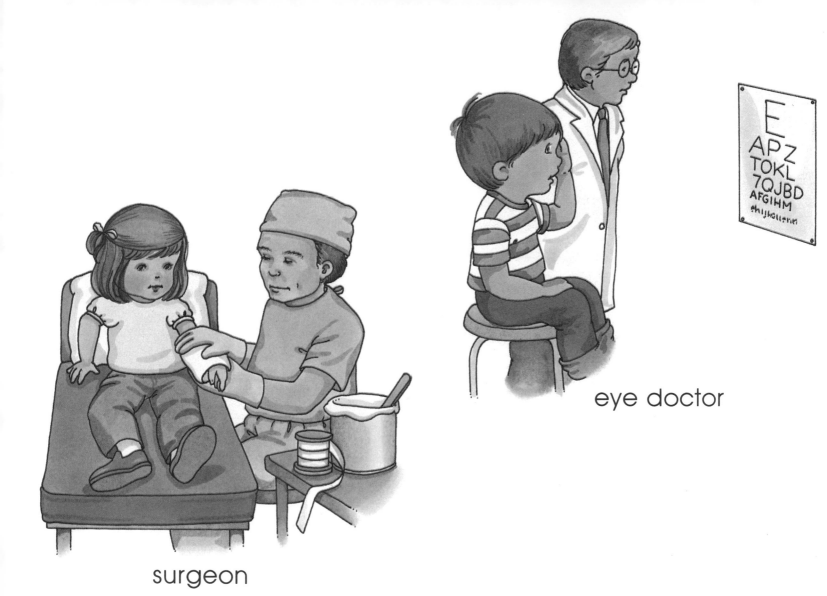

surgeon

eye doctor

well and happy every day.

Look in the box again. What do you see? Can you guess who we will be?

Fix-it people. That's who. What do
fix-it people do?

They fix things. That's what they do.

repairman

carpenter

mechanic

plumber

They fix a roof, a car, or a broken door,
or a broken pipe under a floor.

Look in the box again. What do you
see? Can you guess who we will be?

Mail carriers, that's who. What do
mail carriers do?

They carry letters, postcards, and packages too.

post office

mail truck

mailbox

you

They carry mail from the post office
right to you.

Before we put all these things away,
tell us, who will you be today?
You can play dress-up too.

Lisa closed the word window.

Here are more "people-helpers" you
may wish to dress up as today.

safety patrol
person

newspaper
seller

bus driver